mommy

Mama

MW01152877

daddy

Papa

boy

Junge

girl

Mädchen

1
one

eins

2
two

zwei

3
three

drei

4
four

vier

5 five
fünf

6 six
sechs

7 seven
sieben

8 eight
acht

9

nine

neun

10

ten

zehn

count

zählen

write

schreiben

draw

zeichnen

paint

malen

circle

Kreis

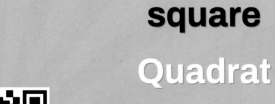

square

Quadrat

rectangle

Rechteck

triangle

Dreieck

star

Stern

black

schwarz

white

weiß

brown

braun

red

rot

blue

blau

yellow

gelb

green

grün

purple

lila

gray

grau

orange

orange

pink

rosa

apple

Apfel

banana

Banane

pineapple

Ananas

watermelon

Wassermelone

pear

Birne

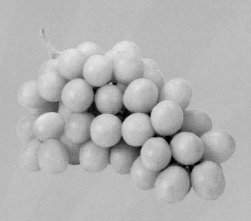

grapes

Weintrauben

mango

Mango

peach

Pfirsich

strawberry

Erdbeere

cherry

Kirsche

orange

Orange

coconut

Kokosnuss

lemon

Zitrone

mushroom

Pilz

corn

Mais

tomato

Tomate

pumpkin

Kürbis

cucumber

Gurke

carrot

Karotte

potato

Kartoffel

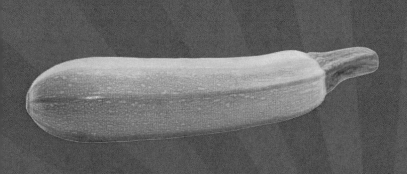

zucchini

Zucchini

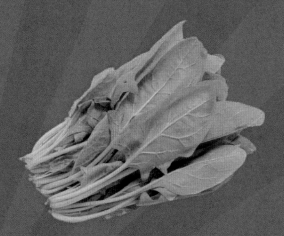

spinach

Spinat

cauliflower

Blumenkohl

egg

Ei

plate

Teller

spoon

Löffel

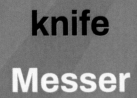

knife

Messer

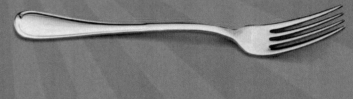

fork

Gabel

cake

Kuchen

baby bottle

Babyflasche

candies

Süßigkeiten

cheese

Käse

drink

trinken

eat

essen

hot

heiß

cold

kalt

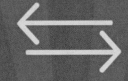 

small

big

klein

groß

short

long

kurz

lang

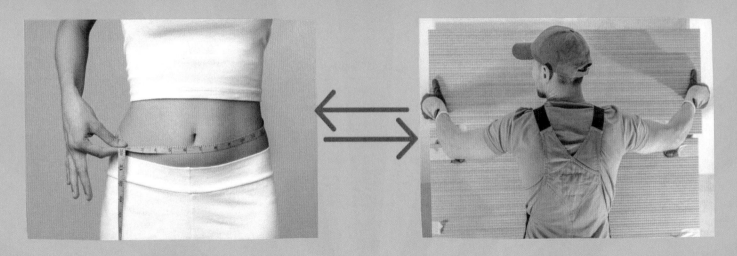

thin

dünn

large

groß

 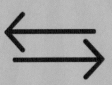 

easy

leicht

difficult

schwierig

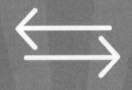

stand up   **sit down**

aufstehen   hinsetzen

sweet   **salty**

süß   salzig

heavy

light

schwer

leicht

in

out

in

aus

dirty

dreckig

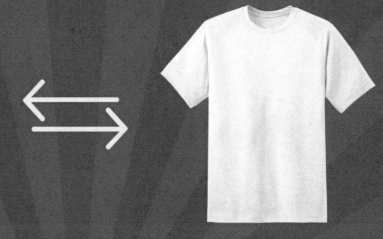

clean

sauber

close

schließen

open

öffnen

pencils

Bleistifte

clock

Uhr

key

Schlüssel

book

Buch

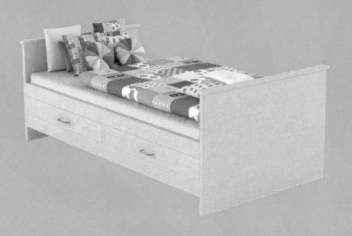

bed

Bett

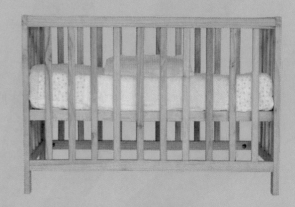

crib

Krippe

table

Tisch

chair

Stuhl

car

Auto

bike

Fahrrad

plane

Flugzeug

boat

Boot

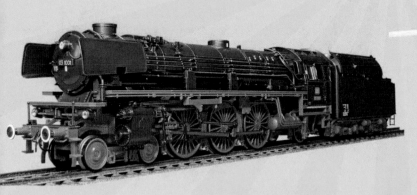

train

Zug

helicopter

Hubschrauber

firetruck

Feuerwehrauto

firefighter

Feuerwehrmann

ambulance

Krankenwagen

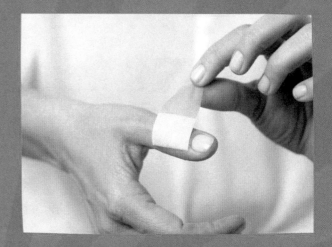

bandage

Verband

paramedic

Rettungssanitäter

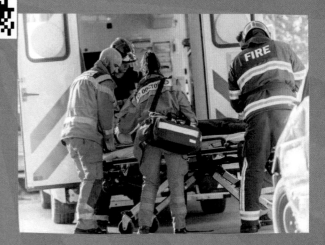

rescue team

Rettungsteam

forest

Wald

mountain

Berg

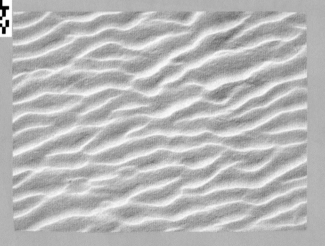

grass

Gras

sand

Sand

tree

Baum

flower

Blume

butterfly

Schmetterling

ant

Ameise

cat

Katze

dog

Hund

horse

Pferd

mouse

Maus

cow

Kuh

pig

Schwein

sheep

Schaf

duck

Ente

goose

Gans

rabbit

Hase

fish

Fisch

vet

Tierärztin

doctor

Doktor

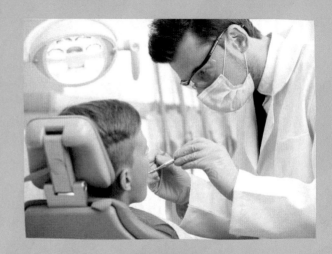

dentist

Zahnarzt

pharmacist

Apotheker

nurse

Krankenschwester

head

Kopf

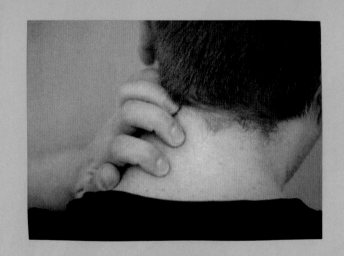

neck

Hals

foot

Fuß

hand

Hand

teeth

Zähne

eye

Auge

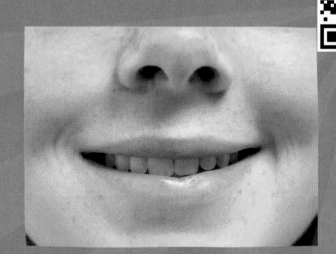

mouth

Mund

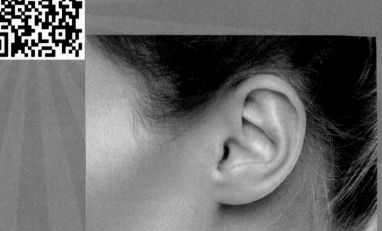

ear

Ohr

hat

Hut

dress

Kleid

pants

Hose

shoes

Schuhe

coat

Mantel

scarf

Schal

umbrella

Regenschirm

glasses

Brille

sun

Sonne

cloudy

wolkig

rainy

regnerisch

moon

Mond

Made in the USA
Middletown, DE
24 July 2024

57943051R00024